Noah's Ark

Written by Bethan Lycett

Illustrated by Hannah Stout

One day Mr Penguin was out for his swim,

when suddenly he heard God was talking to him:

"Call Mrs Penguin, pack up before dark,

and find Mr Noah, who's making an ark."

"An ark?" said the penguin, "But what could that be?"

God said, "It's a boat that he's building for me!

Everyone but Noah is up to no good,

So I have decided to send a world flood."

Off went the penguins, and after a while,

they met Mr and Mrs Crocodile.

Mr Crocodile said God had talked to him too,

and asked what the penguins thought they should do.

"I think we should join up, I saw in a dream.

We'll find Noah together; oh, what a great team!"

A large group of sheep were walking ahead;
fourteen in total, but out they all spread.

Penguin asked God, "Why fourteen, and not two?"

God answered "They're different, I need more than of you.

After the time you will spend on the sea

then they will be food, and an offering to me."

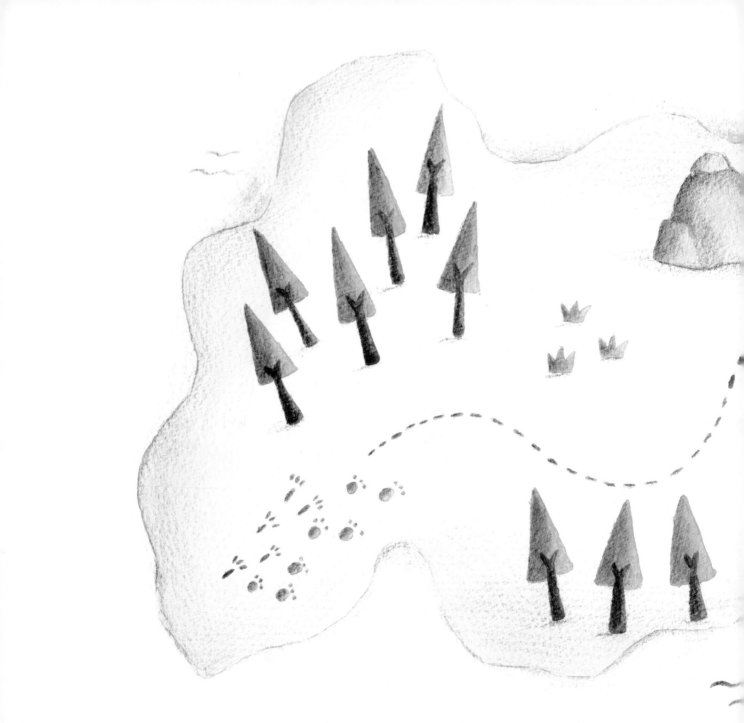

The little group travelled for day after day,

picking up many more friends on the way.

Finally the **animals**
arrived at the **ark**,
Noah was pleased as the
sky had turned **dark**.

"No pushing or shoving, there's room for you all,

no animal too big, and no insect too small.

God's chosen you all for this plan he has made;

now into the ark, and don't be afraid."

Pitter and patter, rain started to fall.

"Away from the door!" Mr Noah did call.

The waters rose quickly, and covered the land,

But inside was safe, just like God had planned.

For forty whole days and forty whole nights

the rain came down, and no end was in sight.

But Noah and his sons took such special care

of all of the animals sheltering there.

For almost a year they all stayed on board.

All that they needed, Noah had stored.

Finally one day the ark came to rest

on top of the mountain God had thought best.

How would they know if the land was all dry?

They needed an animal, one that could fly.

All the birds gathered at Noah's request.

Noah picked Raven to seek out a nest.

Raven just flew about over the sea.

Next, Noah sent Dove and he found a small tree.

When Dove went out later he never came back,

so Noah then knew it was time to unpack.

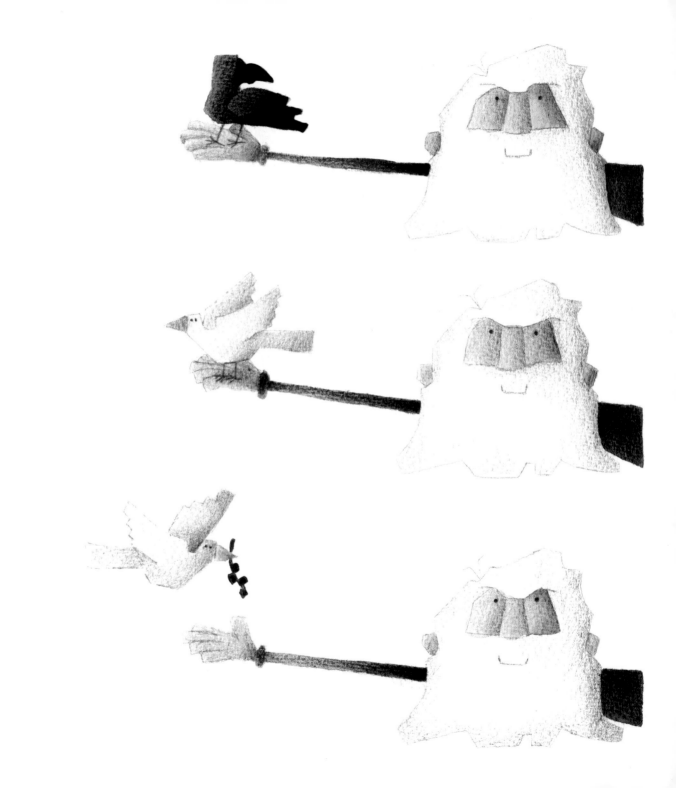

The door was swung open, the land was now dry,

the animals were leaving and saying goodbye.

Then God, he blessed Noah, and put him in charge

of all of the animals, tiny and large.

God **promised** that never again would there be
a **flood** over all of the **earth** and the **sea**.
To help us **remember** the promise God made,
he sent us a **rainbow**, so we won't be afraid.

God made a way for Noah to be saved on the ark, and God has made a way for us to be saved, through Jesus dying on the cross.

One day Jesus will come and judge the world and those who have asked Jesus to forgive them for the wrong things they have done will have a new start with Him, which can never be spoiled, in Heaven.

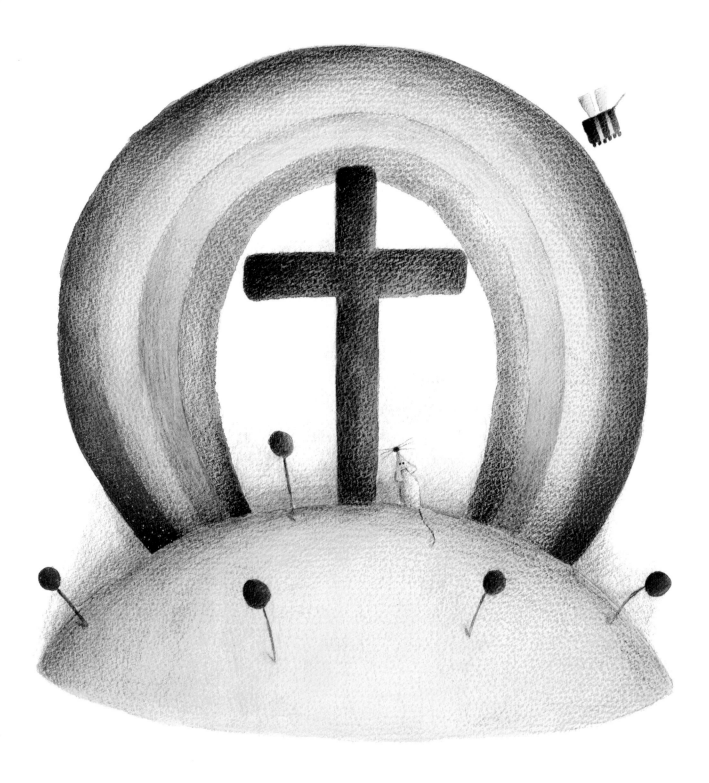

In the Bible, in 1 John 4 v 14, it says...

"We have seen with our own eyes

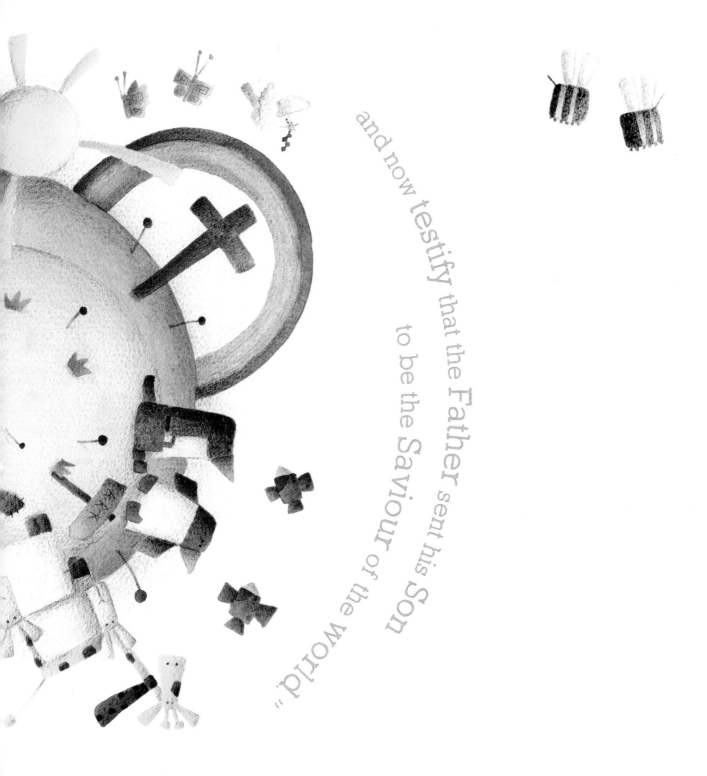

and now testify that the Father sent his Son to be the Saviour of the world."

Joel, Lily, Elsie,
James.

Noah's Ark

Text and Illustrations © 2014. Bethan Lycett and Hannah Stout.

Published by 10Publishing, a division of 10ofThose Limited.
ISBN 978-1-909611-60-3

Design and Typeset by: Diane Bainbridge. Printed in the UK.

10Publishing, a division of 10ofthose.com
9D Centurion Court, Farington, Leyland, PR25 3UQ, England
Email: info@10ofthose.com Website: www.10ofthose.com